Kadupul Flower

poems

Kimberly Vargas Agnese

GREEN WRITERS PRESS | *Brattleboro, Vermont*

Kadupul Flower is a work of fiction. Names, characters, places and incidents either are the product of the author's imagination or are used fictitiously. Any resemblance to actual persons, living or dead, events, businesses, companies, or locales is entirely coincidental.

Printed in the United States.

10 9 8 7 6 5 4 3 2 1

Green Writers Press is a Vermont-based publisher whose mission is to spread a message of hope and renewal through the words and images we publish. Throughout we will adhere to our commitment to preserving and protecting the natural resources of the earth. To that end, a percentage of our proceeds will be donated to environmental and social-activist groups. Green Writers Press gratefully acknowledges support from individual donors, friends, and readers to help support the environment and our publishing initiative.

green writers press

Giving Voice to Writers & Artists Who Will Make the World a Better Place
Green Writers Press | Brattleboro, Vermont
www.greenwriterspress.com

ISBN: 979-8-9914134-4-2

COVER ART: RUSHDA @CLEANPNG.COM

PRINTED ON RECYCLED PAPER BY BOOKMOBILE.
BASED IN MINNEAPOLIS, MINNESOTA, BOOKMOBILE BEGAN AS A DESIGN AND TYPESETTING PRODUCTION HOUSE IN 1982 AND STARTED OFFERING PRINT SERVICES IN 1996.
BOOKMOBILE IS RUN ON 100% WIND- AND SOLAR-POWERED CLEAN ENERGY.

For my daughter Stephanie, who believes in Him . . . and who has believed in both me and my poetry more than anyone else this side of Heaven.

Kadupul Flower

poems

Kimberly Vargas Agnese

GREEN WRITERS PRESS | *Brattleboro, Vermont*

Kadupul Flower is a work of fiction. Names, characters, places and incidents either are the product of the author's imagination or are used fictitiously. Any resemblance to actual persons, living or dead, events, businesses, companies, or locales is entirely coincidental.

Printed in the United States.

10 9 8 7 6 5 4 3 2 1

Green Writers Press is a Vermont-based publisher whose mission is to spread a message of hope and renewal through the words and images we publish. Throughout we will adhere to our commitment to preserving and protecting the natural resources of the earth. To that end, a percentage of our proceeds will be donated to environmental and social-activist groups. Green Writers Press gratefully acknowledges support from individual donors, friends, and readers to help support the environment and our publishing initiative.

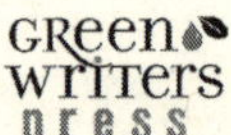

Giving Voice to Writers & Artists Who Will Make the World a Better Place
Green Writers Press | Brattleboro, Vermont
www.greenwriterspress.com

ISBN: 979-8-9914134-4-2

COVER ART: RUSHDA @CLEANPNG.COM

PRINTED ON RECYCLED PAPER BY BOOKMOBILE.
BASED IN MINNEAPOLIS, MINNESOTA, BOOKMOBILE BEGAN AS A DESIGN AND TYPESETTING PRODUCTION HOUSE IN 1982 AND STARTED OFFERING PRINT SERVICES IN 1996.
BOOKMOBILE IS RUN ON 100% WIND- AND SOLAR-POWERED CLEAN ENERGY.

ADVANCE PRAISE FOR *KADUPUL FLOWER*

"Kimberly Vargas Agnese is a true seer. The people who populate *Kadupul Flower* are given full color and dignity in poem after graceful poem. This marvelous book is engaged with its community and the justice it deserves, honoring the culture and the land along the way. Fresno comes alive: concrete, canal, chochoyote. We're reminded that 'nobody owns the sky.' I *love* this book."

—LEE HERRICK, California Poet Laureate

"*Kadupul Flower* is a poetic memoir and a call for 'whole' interconnection with nature, ancestors, family, self and migrant realities in the San Joaquin Valley. It is also a flow of kindness, cultural search, and familia harmony. An exquisite, tender tapestry of our lives: bold realities in the Valley, on earth, within nature and beyond. ¡Viva Kimberly Vargas Agnese!"

—JUAN FELIPE HERRERA, MacArthur Fellow
and United States Poet Laureate Emeritus

"*Kadupul Flower* is as strong and sensitive as the blossoms of forgiveness and hummingbirds of hope discovered in these poems. A beautiful and powerful collection."

—MARGARITA ENGLE, Young People's Poet
Laureate Emeritus
and Author of *Wild Dreamers*

Praise for THERE IS NEWS ALONG THE OHIO RIVER

"In Beth Gilstrap's *There Is News Along the Ohio River*, daily walks along the Ohio's 'borderland of metal, earth, and water' become essential acts of survival. The speaker at a brink, the country at a brink, the river reveals herself as mother, refuge, witness, and tether. This collection speaks to the 'pocket between rib and collarbone where so much trauma lives'; which is to say, it speaks vulnerability and tenderness from one who knows. I loved Gilstrap's genre-fluid lyric forms and was profoundly moved by her deep attention to place and psyche."

—VIOLETA GARCIA-MENDOZA, author of *Songs for the Land-Bound*

"In *There Is News Along the Ohio River*, a series of short glimpses reveal the people and the place so deeply that every snippet feels like a novel. In orange sneakers and baked beans and yellow roses, tiny details become windows into the world. This is a tender and beautifully written work, and Gilstrap finds such kindness for humanity that the book feels like the guide we all need right now."

—CHLOE N. CLARK, author of *Every Galaxy a Circle*

"*There is News Along the Ohio River* is a mesmerizing collection about sore hearts, tangled minds, and the art of noticing the natural world. Dreamlike and haunting, these pieces invite us in with sharp details and astonish us with their turns, lingering long after the book is closed, shining with hard-fought truths."

—HEATHER BELL ADAMS, author of *Maranatha Road*

ADVANCE PRAISE FOR *KADUPUL FLOWER*

"Kimberly Vargas Agnese is a true seer. The people who populate *Kadupul Flower* are given full color and dignity in poem after graceful poem. This marvelous book is engaged with its community and the justice it deserves, honoring the culture and the land along the way. Fresno comes alive: concrete, canal, chochoyote. We're reminded that 'nobody owns the sky.' I *love* this book."

—LEE HERRICK, California Poet Laureate

"*Kadupul Flower* is a poetic memoir and a call for 'whole' interconnection with nature, ancestors, family, self and migrant realities in the San Joaquin Valley. It is also a flow of kindness, cultural search, and familia harmony. An exquisite, tender tapestry of our lives: bold realities in the Valley, on earth, within nature and beyond. ¡Viva Kimberly Vargas Agnese!"

—JUAN FELIPE HERRERA, MacArthur Fellow
and United States Poet Laureate Emeritus

"*Kadupul Flower* is as strong and sensitive as the blossoms of forgiveness and hummingbirds of hope discovered in these poems. A beautiful and powerful collection."

—MARGARITA ENGLE, Young People's Poet
Laureate Emeritus
and Author of *Wild Dreamers*

CONTENTS

KADUPUL FLOWER

ORANGE IS SYMBOLIC OF WIRIKUTA

For $4.95, you can get four seedpods at Howard Johnson's,
put them next to a plate of spaghetti, stuff them into your pocket,
whisper "magic" in the backseat of your mom's Nova.

You don't need to know that the bean is not a bean
(or that the larva was born in Sonora
or that your grandmother was a Cortés)
to get the 98% on a history test so Mom will be proud,
or to laugh with your brother when he tells you,
"Get out of the sun, you're getting too dark."

Stomach turning gray like the belly
of a *Laspeyresia saltitans* moth.

So where exactly are we in this whole "Nature vs. Nurture"
debate?

Would it have changed anything if I had known
that orange is symbolic of Wirikuta in Huichol art?

The sacred place where life began, the womb of *mis abuelos*,
the ink above my breasts, the copper threads within my skin—

or that new Wixaritari fathers weave yarn
between two crossed sticks,
praying for babies to see summers

children within grandchildren, marrow within bones.

Fact: If all conditions are optimal, the larva
within a *Hierba de la Flecha* seed
will cut a small circular door, spin a silken cocoon,
waken from winter to lay eggs
in the ovary of an *herb of the arrow.*

So, what happens to the life cycle of the light gray moth
when jumping beans are collected from rocky deserts,
packaged into plastic boxes, shipped across the border,
far from the arroyos of Mexico?

YOU DON'T CHECK THE TEETH

Shifting from foot to foot on the stained sidewalk outside the
  kindergarten gate
Blanca looks for Papa's slate-colored hair and faded blue sleeve
hanging over the window of the Chevy
he drives to the field every day
to pick through hairy vines for juicy red *tomates*
so that they can go to the *supermercado*
and buy corn and beans and *chiles* . . .

"And a *piñata* for my birthday,"
she chirps as she hopscotches
over store tiles, past the old woman whose face
reminds her of the eggs in the refrigerator

where cartons of *horchata*, milk
and other white things are sold to brown ladies
standing under figurines of saints
that the old woman says are charming

until she squints at the dirt under Papa's fingernails:
grit the color of dark water balloons dotting the plum tree
outside the kitchen window where their family eats supper.

Blanca watches the little owls in Papa's eyes swivel
as the stars come out in his mouth to whisper,
"*A caballo regalado, no se le ven los dientes.*"

As he helps the lady with manicured fingernails
find a ripe cantaloupe on the table piled with melons
(next to different shades of bananas),
he pours English into her ears:
"You don't check the teeth of a gifted horse."

When Blanca asks him to explain
he tells her "Someday,"
and looks between her lashes
fluttering like feathers on a crested caracara.

"But I hope you will never have to understand."

RAPE OF THE LAND

She pulls on her boots so she can step over grass
flooded with broken sewer pipes and mosquito larvae

to follow a sunlit cloud of tractor dust
rippling between fences and kitchens
frying *papas con huevos*,

past canals reflecting sparrows and the early morning chatter
of children walking to bus stops

across the field
where she brushes yesterday's exhaustion
and stray weeds off today's hoe

pretends not to notice the guy in the bandana
who is trying to rip her purple hoodie off her body
with his eyeballs

until he smiles at her—

his teeth gleaming like the fishhooks
he uses to catch supper for his *abuelita*

who pats flour and her grandchildren's angry hands:
"Put a good face to the bad times. Be positive."

When he is with his grandmother,
he eats tortillas. His palms grow white.

But when he is not

his teeth chew dust in the farmer's field
and his fingertips weather and split into furrows.

His thoughts fall into cracks where foremen talk on cell phones
and rednecks toss greasy sandwich wrappers
and *go-back-to-Mexico*s out of white-boy trucks.

He clenches his fists
across the row from the girl
(who hunches over in her purple hoodie,
hoeing foxtails)

to keep himself from lunging at her,
from tearing her prickly pear with his teeth,
from ripping the hopeful canals right out of her eyes

on the land where his great-great-grandmother
knelt to gather berries
for her family

before their land was raped.

JUAN RAMÓN VASQUEZ

Resting on the crossbeams of a white picket fence,
a pair of eyes nests above a patch of freckles—
watching children old enough to go to school
pick tomatoes in the field across the canal

Behind her
European starlings plant eggs the color of Mexican bluebirds
in homes woven from borrowed palms
under the eaves of her two-story house,
where she can see her mother watching TV through the window

> "Juan Ramón Vasquez, who has been convicted
> of raping a child, pleaded guilty to illegal entry
> after previously being deported from the U.S."

The driver of a taco truck passes threadbare pockets of field workers
whose fingers smell like uneaten fruit,
backs glistening like gold.

If she squints into the reflection bouncing between the shutters
she can see two women separated by wrinkled asphalt

one sitting on the sofa
making the sign of the cross;
another wiping dust and sweat off the rosary
hanging between her son's shoulders

prayers glistening under the San Joaquin sun:
"Lord God, from You every family
in Heaven and on Earth
takes its name."

OUR INHERITANCE

These blue seas and sobbing coasts,
green webbed stems and voles

meadow crusts and pocketless sunflowers
bending towards the orb

are a kind of gold that wilts
when cut

EATING MONEY

Only when the last tree has been cut down,
the last fish has been caught, and the last stream poisoned,
will we realize we cannot eat money.
CREE PROVERB

My daughter tithes
into the earth.

Doesn't matter if it's 112°.

Stephanie's still going to lean over that bucket pond
to rescue a floundering bee,
sow sweat into the dust next to the six-foot rosemary bush
where bits of sky bloom in winter.

Let water drip through the hose in her hands
to nurse bare roots
bought with stimulus checks.

In Mexico, our ancestors built floating gardens.
But who cares about that?

She should have deposited the money
into her bank account.

Watched the canopy on those checks grow
until they could water the desert.

Acted like an American.

With a future.

KADUPUL FLOWER

What if a trickle of water streams over the lip of my roof,
filters through beaks of year-old doves standing on the edge
of our rain gutter,
instead of from one of those high-end luxury ponds?

On the other side of the good pane,
(the one that doesn't have a dried leaf
taped to a piece of binder paper to cover the crack)
water falls between fingers of Mexican fronds,
warbles over greenery about six feet away from the Bible
which sits on our kitchen table.

With the last $5.48 left on our food stamp card,
I can buy masa and lard to make *chochoyotes* that should
stretch us 'til Thursday.

In Genesis, it says
Let the water under the sky be gathered into a single basin
and *Let the earth bring forth vegetation, every kind of plant that
bears seed.*
But The New York Times says that cuttings from Ecuador
cost $200 a-piece.

I read somewhere that a Juliet rose could cost 15 million.
Everyone buying and selling the Creator's stuff.

Probably not a good idea to plant a Kadupul flower in a
bog garden.

In Mexico, that cactus grows
between tree branches and rock crevices,
considered priceless.

THROUGH THE BARS

A bird wing shadow falls through the bars of my grocery cart,
hovers over the run-off water spilling into the gutter
muddied with broken bottles, a take-out bag
and a used condom flung out of a car window

A throng of shoelaces and white socks pause
at the puddle forming around my bare feet,
high step and cross to the side of the road
where manicured fingers set up lawn chairs
and flimsy signs protesting injustice

I stand up to scrub the spaces between my toes
in the sprinklers watering the shrubs behind me
until the palms of my feet
grow pink above the pulse of the earth

Overhead, an F-16 formation tears through the sky and the
earth trembles

through the shutters of my eyes
I remember Mama inside her kitchen rolling biscuits,
stringing socks on the clothesline next to our vegetable garden

Across the street, little ones bury their heads
    in their mothers' laps;
when the rumbling stops, they whine for for *helados*

My footprints bake unheard in the commercial plot
as I kneel in the grass, looking for feathers
to weave through the dreadlocks surrounding my temples

beneath the wool of my hair,
my face ripens in the sun

MEADOWLARKS

Olivia presses all six years of herself
into the back of the chair
and opens the box of Whoppers
Mama bought for her at the concession stand
where they sell popcorn and sodas

to everyone except the skinny lady outside
who doesn't have any money
so all she gets to do is watch
feathers and feet pick at garbage
under the smoky sky.

Before the feature starts
a boy spills a bunch of popcorn—
enough to fill that hungry woman's beak
and then some

but Mama says,
"Sit and watch the movie."

So Olivia stares at white clouds and wheat fields
until a bird jumps and she has to ask,

"Why is his cheek covered in soot?"

and Mama says,
"That's just a meadowlark.
Don't see as many of those around here as we used to."

Olivia sticks the Whopper,
a malt ball the color of dirt
the shape of the world,
in her mouth

sucks the earth right off it
and says,
"Oh, I forgot."

NOTES FROM A NEIGHBORHOOD MEETING

Everybody knows
that between the cement walls of the Friant Kern canal,
water flows through the San Joaquin Valley, irrigating
farmland

So that's not what we talked about at our last
Neighborhood Association meeting

What concerned us was the homeless guy who lives under
the bridge,
hanging his clothes on a makeshift laundry line

how he climbed over the dilapidated fence boards behind
Mrs. Day's house
to camp out while she was watering her plants one night,
accidentally spraying him

I guess he didn't want to get wet (what with the weather
getting colder, and warmth being so hard to come by)
and being a widow, she couldn't really afford to take up
with a crazy man
running around her yard yelling obscenities

Of course, the sheriff needed to be called
so he could chase the guy to the other side of the tracks,
where homeless people are allowed to exist
if they can make it through the night without being killed

Maybe Phil, whose hair is the color of the streets he sweeps,
was right when he said that it would be nice
if we'd all offer to share our garbage cans with each other

You know, act like neighbors

NAMELESS

You could tell it was him by the clothes he lived in

the T-shirt that was supposed to be white,
now the color of bushes on the side of the bike trail
jeans slack from walking and sleeping,
hard-pressed to use the bathroom, brush his teeth
let alone wash socks (if he has any)
air around him fermenting fruit

but then again, our neighborhood smells like that
when steam puffs out of smokestacks from the winery on
  Clovis Avenue.
Everyone knows about it,
and the meth house on the corner of the street,
the squad cars, the helicopters, the megaphones,
the woman in the white van calling out to anyone who
  will listen,
"*¡tamales, tamales!*"

but we don't know him,
even though we've seen him a hundred times.
He's just the guy who walks up and down Clovis Avenue,
where the old railroad used to run.

Back in the 1930s, my family says, Grandpa was a bum
hopping trains across the country

I wonder how his chin looked in the summer

did he shave
or let it grow like the old weedy beard on this guy
walking underneath canopies of ash trees where even birds
have the right to build nests?

Did he whistle, the skin across his cheeks stretching
like metal on the bed of a high-brow truck
or apologize for climbing over the invisible barbed-wire fence
planted around homeowners' associations?

Did he ever get so tired of being nameless
that he walked up to someone, anyone
a mother, a father, a shop owner
stick out his hand and say,

"Hello. My name is Douglas."

Did they take the tweed of his palm,
look into his eyes,
talk about the weather

or hide behind the twigs around their eyes
until he hid, too
behind the brush on the side of the road,
hugging the home within his ribcage?

I hope to God that didn't happen.

I hope he tipped his hat,
slicked sweat-darkened feathers out of his face

chuckled like a mockingbird, jutted out his chin,
grinned so big they could see each pearl-handled tooth

nodded to say,
"Nobody owns the sky."

WHEN TV LAND IS ON IN THE RESTAURANT

In 2023, it's still thoroughly charming
to watch Wally Cleaver scoop ice cream on TV Land,
Flipper fly off the coast of Florida, and

the homeless woman outside the window
beyond Leave It to Beaver's white picket fence.

Fred and Ethel need three months' rent in advance.

Her blond unwashed hair presses against stucco.

Lucy bets Ricky she can go
without modern conveniences
longer than he can.

I step outside.

On the other side of the stone,
cashiers dole out coins to aprons
frying burgers

before picking up children
demanding Nintendos.

But all Lucy wants
is to dance in Ricky's night show.

"Do you want some of these?"
the homeless woman asks,
like a schoolyard friend
hiding in a concrete tunnel.

From the valley of her palm,
from the kitchen in her hand,
she offers cold french fries.
They could have been Skittles.

I slide down the wall.
Say, "Yes."

ARIANA

Ariana is five, so her parents think
it is time for her to leave the nest
and ride the school bus,

so she climbs those steps and walks down the aisle
but there is not enough room for her backpack
next to the kid sitting by the window
smudged with years of fingers
grasping for tree leaves
just outside the glass.

So she hugs her yellow bag to her heart
until Teacher shows where her name tag is taped
above a set of small boxes.

She can shove her lunchbox and pink sweatshirt into a cubby,
stick her pencils into the dark space inside her desk
and sit there until she learns how to stare at the teacher
instead of the birds flying outside the window.

Someday after lunch,
when she is maybe thirty-three
she will know how to make a name for herself

and where to find it on the row of mailboxes
(in front of her apartment complex)
which sit under a sky the color of a robin's egg,

climb stairs to the door, find her way to the narrow box
in the cupboard where knives and forks are separated
from the plastic wrap

and suffocate.

In the morning,
she will send her daughter to school.

CLIMBING JACK'S BEANSTALK

Back when I was in kindergarten,

beyond the poster of liana vines that looked like they could
be from "Jack and the Beanstalk"
and the kindergarten desks which used to be trees until
they weren't anymore,
plastic cups full of dirt sat on the windowsill, hugging five
magic pea seeds waiting to be born.

Fee fi fo fum . . .

"Do you have your coins?" Teacher asks,
because everyone knows you've got to hold onto your
money
if you want to eat with the big kids at the cafeteria
or the mercenary giants like Suzano and Klabin in South
America.

Their pulp mills chew through 3,000-foot-long vines in
the rainforest
so fifth graders can read about deforestation in that chapter
about global warming.

Fee fi fo fum . . .

Farmers' Almanac says summer here in Fresno is gonna get
hotter.

Last year, feather-picked scrub jays hopped slack-jawed,
gaping at the sun,
red fox squirrels flopped over walnut branches
and I sat by the window, hoping the dragonfly
that usually clutched the long twig next to the pond
was only hiding from the heat and not dead.

Fee fi fo fum . . .

Loggers seize rainforest trees to make their bread.
Sage plunges roots into parched earth,
unwilling to let go.

Guajajara patrol the Arariboia.[1]
Ground bees hover above lavender blossoms,
cling to stalks in the wind . . .

In winter, I will tuck bare roots into dry dirt,
swap coins for envelopes full of seeds,

1 The Guajajara, a tribe indigenous to the Brazilian state of Maranhão, defend the Arariboia region of the Amazon rainforest against loggers.

stock up on cowpeas and cucamelon vines,
stick Malabar spinach and yard-long beans
in the beat-up box next to my kitchen table,
grow a food forest.

Climb Jack's beanstalk,
grab the golden goose . . .

hold onto something good.

RED STRINGS

My toes sweat against the plastic of $0.99 flip-flops
as I scurry across the parking lot and into the grocery store,
around tables piled with strawberries picked by immigrants
up and down familiar aisles, glancing at discounted bags
of already-diced cactus, thumping watermelon.

I stand in line and wait for my favorite cashier
to ask me how I'm doing.

"Hot," I pant.

"What's this? This isn't hot. I grew up in Mexico."

She holds up an aloe vera leaf I plan to put in a smoothie.
"You know, if you tie a red string around this plant,
 it will keep you safe.
But this, it costs too much. Come to my house
 and I will give you some."

Her fingers move quickly,
penning her phone number onto my receipt.
"Call me."

I thank her, then shove the purchases inside a plastic bag,
push the cart out of store-bought air conditioning
and weave back through the parking lot,
sandals flapping like a bird.

I wilt a little as I load the trunk of the SUV where
my daughter sits,
long blonde hair dangling over a berry-stained Bible
the color of her favorite sweater,
of heart stickers on the name tags at her best friend's *quinceañera*,
of salsa served at the orientation for her library tech job out
in Easton.

"A little boy asked for one,"
she says, thumbing through the pages,
"but I'm not sure if I'm allowed to bring it."

She balances the book on her lap and I drive,
because that's what you do when you're on food stamps
and there's not enough money for extra car insurance.

You drive. Back and forth every day,
past fields of migrant workers catching sweat beads in bandanas,
so your daughter can read to children who no longer live in
Mexico,

who work with their parents picking tomatoes after school
and get out of bed before chickens start pecking gravel
on the side of the road.

They pick . . . you drive . . .
she brings a little boy

something red

ON THE WAY TO THE LIBRARY

A satire

That wasn't a pigeon looping skyward in front of my car,
weaving through sunset strips of Aztec-colored threads—
pink, blue, purple,
wingtips gray.

But who cares?

A bird is a bird is a bird, whether it blends into dusk
or pecks corn in an old woman's garden.

But since I'm only driving
(and don't have anything better to do)
let's suppose the woman's hat brim lifts away
from the grease splotches on her apron
and she spots a nest.

It is still only one nest out of millions of nests,
not really important.

On a shelf in a library somewhere,

A freshman pulls an article by Ward Churchill[1]
out of the archives.

But does it really matter whether the U.S. Army
gave smallpox blankets to Indians?

Genocide? I doubt it.
Conspiracy theories.
Fabrications. False.

Just Liberals crying wolf.

Gilroy. El Paso.
Snipers picking off Mexican families
in the school supply aisle
like they're common,
ordinary rock-colored birds.

It wasn't a pigeon,
it was a mourning dove
just flying towards sunrise.

1 Prominent, if controversial, American activist and author of numerous works about the genocide of Indigenous peoples

SITTING IN THE SUN

Out in the country beyond faded picket lines
corralling crepe myrtles, an old gas pump
and an American flag,
I squat in the two by four shadow of my SUV
squinting against sunlight, horse flies and tractor dust.

Across from me,
dirt clods and the rise and fall of a field
detach from the road's shoulder
soldiered by broken palms scattering
fronds and black seeds.

An old pickup slowly stumbles along behind me,
bouncing a sun-ripened elbow and the chirps of a little girl
over edges of rolled-down windows.

"What will you buy me for my *quince, papi?*"
His answer flutters over asphalt,
gets lost in bits of gravel.

Above my ears,
on and around a rough-hewn trunk,

a squirrel's claws clatter,
his palm-colored body pinioned sideways.

He ducks down onto the floor of his semi-desert,
around slender tree shadows
broken across waiting furrows
sectioning the field into flags.

A hot wind blows mirages of mismatched birds
towards Route 1 where the Pacific Ocean crashes
just short of coastal redwood threads
bent in prayer.

AFTER THE AFTERNOON FALLS TO ITS KNEES

I never looked at the 16-year-old's bike.
Black eyes, brows and hair.
Pale face. Too young to drive a car.

Our Chevy is in the parking lot behind dirt plots
where bougainvilleas climb around doorways.
Abuelitas grow dahlias and lemon verbena.
Opium petals sway on the tall green stalks
lining the path that leads to our apartment.

"Wait, what?"

"It's a good thing for your husband
the Bulldogs aren't here anymore."

"Did they bother you?"

Head nods back like he's drinking a Slurpee.
"No, I'm half Mexican.
They wouldn't bother you, either."

We stand in the shadow tree clump
across from the projects' blank-eyed windows
where laundry lines dangle
above communal grass

and the long, hot asphalt strip is dry as a stream bed
that's forgotten rain.

After the afternoon falls to its knees, the sky grows dark.

Cesar Chavez says a prayer
and we stand in the shower of the stars.

PATIENT EARTH

I don't drive in a fetal position
when I steer this car over the patient earth,
painted with tar pitch.

Don't want to run over the old lady in the floral dress
stepping off the curb to scowl at grasshoppers
in her neighbor's flower garden.

Across the way is the church where we vote on Election Day,
where you can see the backs of suit-clad men
checking boxes in a booth—
bet they check "yes" for road repair initiatives.

The street parts hair-like strands of meadow weeds
and a yellow finch sways on a wild mustard stem
blowing from the wind behind my wheels.

I imagine follicles of wild green grass plastered under tar,
small, matted shoots; white roots—
the gravel on the side of the road trembling in homage
to waves of busses taking kids home from school.

Somewhere under Coke bottles and asphalt,
the earth waits . . .

catching sunbeams in hopeful cracks.

MIGRANTS

Just like today,

back in the '60s, people threw bottles
of root beer out their windows
when the highway patrol wasn't looking.

So whether or not anyone liked it, there was probably
more glass on the side of Highway 99
outside the shack where the black Okie slept
than hung between the ceiling slats
of his one-lightbulb home.

Oh go down, Moses
Way down into Egypt's land.

North of Jim Crow
smack dab in the middle of California's Central Valley
where he had hoped to plant children and dreams
between rows of onions and broken promises,
the migrant farm worker shovels long hours
before the stars in his daughter's mouth begin to sing:

A Dios rogando y con el mazo dando
Praying to God and working the mallet hard.

Chickens still peck at glassy-eyed ginger ale bottles
in the gravel next to the field where he gathers dust
  between his teeth—
plants worry sharp as glass in the furrows between his eyes

Hierba mala nunca muere
Weeds never die.

AN ARBITRARY HISTORY OF FLORA AND FAUNA IN FRESNO

Indigenous slaves and ash trees,

Fort Miller
William Helm
Savage River
Stanford
Pacific Railroad
Chinatown
Subdivisions
Streetcars
German farms
Armenian orchards
County courthouse
Kearney Mansion
Italian vineyards
The Fresno Bee
William Saroyan
Azteca Theater

Illegal Indigenous deported

Concrete

PLATFORM SHOES

"Excuse me, ma'am, are you registered to vote?"

That time again.

Bargain bin petitions,
sunflowers, lavenders
and that spreading Greek oregano
that doesn't get very tall.

Last year's seed packets four for a dollar.

Come February, I want to see sweet pea blossoms all over
that arch
my daughter and I pretend is the entrance to Bilbo the
hobbit's house.

A red, white and blue T-shirt marked down to $2.99,
a toy gun, a rainbow-colored scarf. Pocket change
for a platform.

Wonder if these seeds are still good.
Sure they are.
Won't know unless I get some.

Gotta fix the twine on the "Baggins" sign
scrub jays shredded planting
dried corn between jute and rust.

Artichoke seeds.

Obama's face on a plate,
Bush, Kennedy, Nixon. Go figure.

I guess the emperor's got new clothes.
Meatloaf seasoning, anyone?

Had to dig down three feet last summer
so we could stand up all the way
when we walked under that trellis.

"Underground entrance to all things Tolkien"
sounds a whole lot better than,
"Didn't think to measure that old cattle panel
before pounding garden stakes in 104° weather."

Gotta plan this stuff out.

Can't put artichokes in front of the pond
stocked with rosy reds
or we won't be able to see the fish.

Literary translation bested literal,
but the sunflowers have still gotta go
behind the Greek oregano.

Biggest in the back, shortest in the front.

Pay the cashier her money.
"Would you be interested in signing
one of these petitions today?"

Smile but shake my head.

"Just trying to earn a living, ma'am."
I know. And everyone with a platform
is just trying to see above the crowd.

But I'm tired.

A trellis is only a tunnel
if it doesn't knock
your daughter's forehead off.

LEMON THORNS

My daughter and I live under a tough sky.

Mini drones do surveillance for the drug house on the
    corner,
tricolored blackbirds swarm like bats at dusk
and when the 144th Fighter Wings cast their shadows,

everything just stops.

The song of the chat evaporates,
feathers in the birdbath still, and the bluejays hide
between lemon tree thorns until the warbirds pass.

After

I'll dig Bermuda grass out from under that tree
(maybe someday we'll have cherries)
throw the long stems in the pile on the patio
so doves can thread weeds into nests.

BET IT'S GOT A TAIL

Left faucet: cold. Right: warm.

Next to the phone on the kitchen table,
the wall squeaks, paper-cut sharp.

Could be a bird perching
on an electrical wire behind the beams—
but who believes stuff like that anymore?

2020, we did.
That's what we like to say.
Never saw it coming.

(Bet it's got a tail.)

Before he died, Granddad
pushed a string back and forth
through a Folgers coffee lid
to make the can squeak.
Over-rosined in the key of E.

But it wasn't a mouse.

(Oh, come on. Speak softly
and carry a big stick.)
Bash the four-foot spider web
above the green picket fence—
even though it's just a purple asparagus frond.

(Bet it's a rat.)

Tried three times to spell "myopia."
Finally looked it up . . .

Think it looks like this.

MIDTERM RESULTS 2022

Can't see the Bermuda grass
through our steamed-up kitchen window,
almost December pale.

Grasping.
Easy to trip over.

Want to yank it out.
Plant some lavender.

CLEARING OUT THE CHERRY TOMATOES

I wouldn't say the hardpan in Fresno melts at the end of January
when stale toast light blurs like the fur of an Australian Shepherd
pressing through that fence the English walnut tree
makes with her twigs, holding hope-waiting clouds,

but it sure looks like the dew has been soaking
those pink-white buds of someday peaches
over in that grass patch,

licking dew drops like little kids
trying to catch snowflakes
on their tongues.

ANNA

I can't talk to you about how our Anna apple tree
stands next to the strawberry hill in our backyard
without selling her soul to the devil
in the details.

Sometimes a forest swallows a tree.

She is a pink and white presence,
without demand

whose branches hold more air
than they did last spring.

If I pick her blossoms with my eyes
or let them fall through my lashes,
it will not matter.

Still, she will stand.

A peaceful bouquet in stark contrast
to a world wearying my senses,
all Goldilocks could ever want.

Neither too hot, nor too cold.

STRONG AS FLOWERS

America seeps into sidewalk cracks,
seeps red graffiti like petals of voices—
unheard

seeps protests
burning white hot
as hell's collection bills

and red as pounds of flesh
stolen from blue-clad officers
attacked by moonlight.

We bleed by candlelight

flicker, wane
and pray

for fishes and loaves
forgiveness and love
to drip like beads of wax

Pray for bandages
white as moonlight

Through tear-stained glass windows,
we light candles. . .

cry for grace as green as trees,
forgiveness as strong as flowers

GENTLE VOICES QUESTIONING

What was that you wanted to know?

I guess the sky was pale blue
like the scrubs the hygienist always wears
over her white turtleneck
when she cleans your teeth.

At least that's what I remember,
coasting home after teaching seventh and eighth graders all
day . . .

The way the white and turquoise colors
pressed above the dash of my car.

The talk show host and the guy who just called in—
Liberals and Conservatives arguing,
demanding answers.

Everyone talking too much,
no one saying enough.

A global warming bumper sticker lunging too close
to the grille of that really big truck two lanes over

both going too fast
and then not fast enough.

Tires screeching,
headlights swerving

four-wheel drive
breaking all the rules in my head—
slashing across dotted lines

smashing expectations
into perpendicular questions.

What do I do / how long before it hits / how bad
is it gonna hurt / am I about to see Jesus /
what about my children / why?

Gray, spinning black . . .

The hands of a nurse just off her shift.
A policeman, silencing the radio.

Gentle voices questioning,
"Are you okay?"

Lifting my eyes to where traffic parted
without the sound of a siren
to where cornflowers grow
on the side of the road

like white clouds in a blue sky

I look at the faces of Heaven
from my stretcher.

I, THE BODY C(H)ORAL

I, the wineskin
multiple

chemical kinetic electrical thermal
Storm
of one

Mammalian constellation
follicular roots microbial clouds
synthetic identities

authentic saliva
chemical cleansing
Molars and Nails

An adhesion of c(h)oral stars

HUMMINGBIRDS ON WIND

Our feathers torn through sieves
like dust

yet breathe upon
our fallen dust

and we will rise
and wing again

and rise above the sieves
again

hummingbirds
on wind

ACKNOWLEDGEMENTS

"You Don't Check the Teeth" from *In the Garden* (2022) appears courtesy of Torrey House Press.

"Juan Ramón Vazquez" first appeared in *SHIFT: A Publication of MTSU Write* (Fall 2020).

"Eating Money" first appeared in *Snapdragon: A Journal of Art and Healing* (Summer 2024).

"Nameless" first appeared in *Common Ground Review* (Fall/Winter 2025).

"Patient Earth" first appeared in *SHIFT: A Publication of MTSU Write* (Fall 2022).

"Lemon Thorns" first appeared in *unstamatic: Newsprint* (October 2022).

"Gentle Voices Questioning" first appeared in *The Purpled Nail: A Journal of the Sacred in the Ordinary* (April 2020).